THE SHORT DRIVE HOME

Also by Joe Osterhaus

The Domed Road, in *Take Three: AGNI New Poets Series: 1*, 1996

Radiance, 2002

THE SHORT DRIVE HOME

Poems by Joe Osterhaus

*Winner of the 2016 Louise Bogan Award
for Artistic Merit and Excellence*

Copyright © Joe Osterhaus 2017

No part of this book may be used or performed without written consent from the author, if living, except for critical articles or reviews.

Osterhaus, Joe
1st edition.

ISBN: 978-0-9965864-5-0
Library of Congress Control Number: 2016914732

Interior Layout by Lea C. Deschenes
Cover Design by Dorinda Wegener
Cover Photo: "George Washington Bridge, New York" by Berenice Abbott
    (American, 1898 – 1991), 1937. Digital image courtesy of the Getty's Open Content
    Program. File Source available upon request.
Editing by Terry Lucas and Tayve Neese

Printed in Tennessee, USA
Trio House Press, Inc.
Ponte Vedra Beach, FL

To contact the author, send an email to tayveneese@comcast.net.

For Alison and Will

Table of Contents

I

The Aughts	3
The White Oak in the Storm	5
Watering at Night	6
The Riverboat	8
Skylight	9
The Slush Pile	11
Food Lion, Winchester, Tennessee	17

II

Election	21
Wildest Hour	22
The Community Garden	25
The Green Banks of the River	27
Eden	29
Library of Alexandria	31
The Short Drive Home	32
The Rose Farm	38

III

Three-Card Monte	43
Next	44
Immigrant Song	46
Two Sticks and a Cake	49

Peterborough	50
Thirst	52
The Bar	56
Rule	58

IV

Smell of the Lamp	63
Reunion	64
Sol	65
Georgetown	68
The Black Oak in the Storm	70
The Parkway	71
Song	77

Notes and Dedications	79
Acknowledgments	81

And why should the sea maintain its turbulence, its elegance,
And draw a film of muslin down the sand
With each receding wave?

—Louis MacNeice

I

The Aughts

Open a cross-beam door
on 13- or 1505;
touch up the hawks' tails in the script
hedging a king's reprieve

of the one-time tenants, who, dispossessed,
still owed him their rent in full.
Some centuries rattle open, with
an off note, not a peal.

The first years may be trough years,
when guards in skeleton coats
heap sandbags, and a riverwall
veins, where a trash barge floats;

when drought papers the countryside
and aphids catch like frost
in crops, that, dying, spread pointillist leaves
in fields of interest.

The future, buckled with stars,
may cut bow waves like a ship
that bound with white static in a wake
whose far edge ribbons the map;

whose lace reversals knit the froth
with misplaced premises
and brace our better intentions with
a new moon's bale of floss.

If the sea drowns the Alps;
or runs in foaming vents
in half-coves, near containment walls
that bank raw elements;

or blisters like the spent fuel rods
that, dropped in echoing mines,
tick down, as the millennia
leaf in chill red veins;

those possibilities—
forked; apparitional—
will jar the meaningless signatures
antennas cut on hills,

while smashed blue vials, all blear and taint,
so fasten the mind
on money, that the chipped green paint
of a park bench will seem coined.

Now CCTV'd streets
cloud on the spinning drives
that ripped our days like cigarette foils
from '03, '04, '05

when carriers packed with body bags
left small tracks on the seas;
lights barbwired the capitals;
and bombers cracked the skies.

The White Oak in the Storm

When the storms come, they rear back, as the light
   coarsens, green as a tide pool's nibs of glass.
     Swept by barreling drafts that print the grass,
their branches roll a whale's back to the net

of rain, and, large-grained in the thunder, quail
   as a stray brand of lightning clarifies
     and checkerboards a path shot through with ice
down which the bolt, like a waterswept flail,

strobes, and a shock white excess twigs and pours.
   Struck, they split and die almost at once—
     live sap charged to pewter in their veins—
and char at every knot as the bolt's course

devours even the leaf tips, singeing wet air.
Downed wires nip downed branches as the skies clear.

Watering at Night

Next door a rain bird, sprung to life, soon draws
sparrows off trash cans as the nearest boughs
rasp a loose downspout. Where the reels collapse,
the rash lace of the water devours its gaps
and sputters, loud as fry fat, on the hot walk;
spotting a crooked hopscotch on the brick.

From your back porch, the sprays lanced through a bed
force blue perennials to kneel in mud
in heavy sequence; and, at your lawn's edge,
tear in irregular droplets on a hedge
that catch light, with your notice; brim; and fall,
still shining, in a dirt pile pebbled with oil.

As you uncoil the hose, drab silhouettes
lean in the curt clay views of satellites:
catwalk and trestle; ramp and ochre hill
now cloud-obstructed sets, now tracks that mill
with shadows: men and women, who, stepped indoors,
channel their desolations through a course

of blueprints or green empties, looped with twine.
As the hose gasps, reflected credits line
a whirlpool of potpourri between two chairs.
The wind stalls in a birch, and, reined in, tears
freshets that score the silver in each leaf.
When the wind resumes, branches lash and drive

your thought from its loose footing in the dark
and ornament the rain bird's trailing arc
with petals, milled in weak verticals; their green
various as the lives cropped from the mean
in real time, as the rain bird ticks on its stand.
Who knew you'd follow such a light command.

The Riverboat

In search of that plug-nickel, one-in-a-million
chance, whose obverse dulls the parking lots with
rain, we board at a riverside pavilion.
Mincing from its stall; fighting its bit with

whited eyes, a colt rears at a gate.
The silvered lenses spread across the stands
flash as the bunched-up pack turn down the straight,
ears pricked as they maneuver through the mounds

of dirt churned like the bet slips in our wake.
As a surge wraps the hull, rock shallows hiss
with the long swells, and coasters, mirrored, snake
over rails derelict as consciousness,

whose loops dint the cold riverfront with glare.
Cries thin as gold leaf settle on thin air.

Skylight

Look, and what may be satellites appear
in even a noon sky;
quaking, as their positions in the clear
evade the eye;

hallucinatory, then diamond-backed
as sharp stones in a stream
or embers from a wildfire blown whistling
through tamarack and elm.

Stirred by the clouds' unlikely tenses,
our planet empties: park and roof
chalked on grained paper; gaunt fences'
accordion wire like a ruff

past which thin figures halt, and mill;
their motions, painted out,
rutting a track wound on a hill
black loudspeakers instruct.

Such heights, drawn through our monitors,
model the sun's decline
in clays that, spooned out from its course
over billboard and ravine

heap at the ends of towns, where pipe organ
substations blot the stars
and tranches of pinwheeling argon wrap
parlors in faint uproar.

When dawn lifts discount skies off racks,
container ships in rows
void ballast waters that speckle the locks
pink as the bedded rose

of distant canyons, ramped with fire,
where tumbrils, raked with smog,
drop lopsided rolls of razor wire
coiled to bite dew from fog.

Yet nowhere can the eye reclaim
the inward settling weight
of the day, brisked by a tedium,
you first walked through a gate

that now, from on high, appears a gap
pinned by a loose-jointed mast
where tourists shake out the same tri-fold map
and the blue kites from your past.

The Slush Pile

1

If torn, hand-written envelopes announced
the unsolicited, much hoped-for work,
then the worn shop truths were also true enough:
the worse the manuscript, the more berserk
        their soon-pronounced
demands for paperback percentages
even John Jakes wasn't earning at the time.
Some of them still stand out: the poet who'd
composed an Arthurian epic in meter and rhyme

whose Lancelot and Guinevere first kissed
as Arthur fought a dragon king. Dying,
the king revealed to Arthur in a mist
his young wife with her lover; crying
        with pleasure as
'she knew another's body at the root.'
Arthur died of grief, and his knights drank
to planting and the dry whisk of the loom.
The poet sent originals, with scuffed pink

erasures burnishing the onionskin.
I skimmed the antique copper of his phrasing, dashed
a few words on a rejection slip,
and put it out of mind, till a line flashed
        on the office phone,
tripped by a panicking receptionist.
A man 'not in the book' had tried to call
an editor, then appeared, and wouldn't leave.
So I slipped down the stair, in whose bright well

I heard, then saw, the poet: a white-haired man
entreating the blue glass. 'You hadn't touched
the pages, or my note; there's not much time . . .'
Leading him out, I thought that he, dispatched,
      would return alone
to the site of the dragon king's death in the Shenandoah;
garden plot mulched with grasshopper wings
and burst, overripe scallion and red pepper;
daylight pushed through the blinds as through a syringe

just boiled in a ticking saucepan on the stove;
tables bent with filigree; framed prints
warped hard against their monochrome by dust
and oil; Royal typewriter with winged vents;
      clean white trove
of onionskin. And was I wrong? His verse
was more than competent; his dialogue,
though archaic, was well-paced; and far worse
epics strafe the brown shires of the catalog.

2

Flip an old switch, and mercury spirits
current between two brittle contact points
that, grimed with spark, busily connect
infinitesimals till a lamp glints
      or a fan worries bits
of ticking in a sparkling column of dust.
So the past carved new channels on the day
we viewed a house beneath a river cliff
on a north fork of the Shenandoah. Clay

in the bluejacketed shallows harpstrung the shadow
cast from a crumbling mill. Above that ruin,
on the cliff's face, pocketed by blast caps for
their knotted stone, black foliations shone
      in a frayed row;
featureless sentries behind the house, from which
the plashing current shook its glittery cell.
I saw him there, in a room below the cliff;
working his stanzas as pebbles skipped and fell.

3

Another writer sent hand-written lists
of her collected works; lists that drifted right
in intimate connection with the brain.
Folded in thirds, creases lined with light,
      those thumb-bitten posts
blocked out titles in the hundreds: tracts on death,
investing, gardening, elections, race;
with short, exclamatory titles, such as
Prose to Cure Woes, or *Meteors: God's Hidden Face*.

Her block print cover letters said she saw
Christ each night in a surplice on her dresser top;
some plight or vision having placed him on
a lace doily backed by a shaving cup
      and sufficient awe—
the odd one in a building, who commandeered
the book swap in the entryway, and strove
to name the birds whistling at dusk. The Parkinson's
trembling in her signature spoke of

the pee stench in the close air of the hall.
The Christ who stood before her mirror won't reveal
the tenderness that burrowed through her work;
his face, the metallic green of a public zeal,
      pitched a low wall
round her understanding of the whole
her drifted lists intuited. Her past
is sealed off now; what end-of-life award
will separate her ambition from its haste?

How soon will a grant office or theorist
reinvent her for another age,
or pull her work from a collapsing slope
in a landfill or a niece's garage,
        or solve the least
of her steel patchwork of conspiracies;
wincingly impermanent as sun off ice?
The soft-edged lion on a pedestal
still eyes the vacancies

she walked after her book club Tuesday nights;
when, excited or enraged by what they'd said
she spoke out in the street light's tin exposure,
swatting at the summer flies that swarmed her head
        year round. Those mites
playing havoc with her notes on metaphor,
she dropped her notebook in her bag. *No rush.*
Backlit gold and saffron in the shop displays
printed a royal excess on the slush.

4

Part through inattention, part through design,
I waited till I thought them safely dead
to write this out. If pity condescends,
then help write their ambition in its stead
      from the curved line
of our footpath along the river, where the chase
still channels the thrashing water toward the bay
and the high wheel cut through the storybook panels
with such dark, roiling chatter in the spray.

Food Lion, Winchester, Tennessee

From here, the line seems not to move at all;
back beneath a clock that diamonds the hours
with blushing vents of coke. At last, we crawl
forward, just as Tess, the salesclerk, lowers
her chin and yanks her cash drawer from the register;
      then taps out the short stacks
  of rust-green twenty-dollar bills.
              Her sub attacks
the bottles of a woman who won't look at her;
who tilts and prods a pin pad with a stylus.

Night sways at the lit boundary of the lot.
Downroad, a Lotto billboard dances with flies,
whose reels card strands of glare, and epaulet
a gambler shaking the bias from two dice
and a drum sunk in the embankment, gouged with rust.
      Inside, the clockwork mists
  track Raleigh's world: from a field
          of broad leaves, twists
of cured tobacco; and, from harbors gigged with rest,
a waxwork queen wept on a waxwork shield.

Once past a bivouac of pans and tents
the new arrivals check their pace, outmatched.
Wheels corkscrewing, they stop for condiments
and, by their ribbons, show the troops dispatched
to stations in the crescent gulf are family
      to some; acquaintances
  to many more. And those absences,
          drawn out so long,
weigh in their words and eyes. Though I chose differently,
who'll say for all of us: we're not that strong?

II

Election

Like blades of grass, the stories we've all heard
about the past lives of a candidate
redden the moonlit bunting, as a crowd
surges forward; then wither in the light

of morning, when a war hero appears
hunched, in handheld footage, on a red crest;
his men shouting as he trembles and stares
at a camp torn by the halo of a blast.

This new man stammers, buffeted by rounds
of newsprint sprayed like shot from canisters
yet will not hold a vigil at the mounds,
nor shout back to the evening broadcasters

or to a world still divided, still ravenous,
the battle was a fire; and his men, blades of grass.

Wildest Hour

1

Camera slung over your shoulder like a pack;
face animated by the troubling glow
of storm surge, as the waves pile in, and black
turrets of water pound what only the locals know

was a paradisal stretch of sand the day before—
you love a storm, and, prompted by the news,
drive through gusts of white rain to the shore
to greet the goose-stepping whitecaps as they sluice

inland, uprooting trees, broadcasting waves
that drown the lower footpaths, and bare rock
whose base recedes and swoons in crooked caves—
you love it, and coax your car onto a dock

next to a sea-green clam shack to drink it all in—
and, never hurt, you'll brave it all again

when any hurricane or nor'easter
flashes, first in the news, then in the sky;
splintering trees to kindling like a twister;
ripping slate roofs off their timbers. Just *why*,

you've never said. Something about a boy's rage
given violet, day-long dominion, dressed in cloud;
about arrowing flocks whose panic cuts a page
from a drowned book whose characters jump red

as brake lights; about your own place as your map
tears in the wind, and you crouch down and snap
quick rolls of film. Edged by the waves, each shot
rolls, luminous with tumult, when you cut

the blanched exposures, red lit with darkroom sun;
and chase a fine edge to the breakers' run.

2

In its wildest hour, when the storm howls tiers
of red sand from the pylons on the shore,
fresh plyboard spatters with haphazard scuts
of rain; and clouds, their shapes cut on the sea,
pour through a diorama screened with wind.
In an abandoned schoolyard, sprigs of ivy
peel back and tear from root-threaded tablets, where doves

lift through a puff-cheeked storm, and trail a sun
in crescents of black motes between the clouds—
sun that bends to dabble its face in green
shallows, near the bared white shoulder of a sandbar.
Delinquent, your awe mixed with recklessness,
you park on a rain-skirted lot, as wind shouts
lines off the panels crashing in the harbor.

The storm surge, for a while, may seem a home;
and a lens ripped from your hand may crack a pane
high on a tower that had seemed invulnerable;
whose floors kick in the mile-high drafts, and lean.
Next to a boarded, sea-green shack, revel
in yourself in selflessness, and snap
the leaning combers till they lift and curl

in red safelight, off gravid photographic stock . . .
    impossible to know what someone feels.
The storm wrack, twisted with the sea's uses,
is as foreign; its hammer dulcimer
of snapped cables and xylophoned roof tiles
tangled with print outs from some agency;
with Neptune's pale flowers, torn from the vast deep.

The Community Garden

Who will contest the greenflies' claim
to fruit peels, curdled bacon, glue?
Narrowing, instant, a snapshot's frame,
clapped shut, erases them from view;

and still those red-eyed griffins chafe
snowberries on a crimson bush—
a negative would light those rough
attentions with its harrier flash.

The garden fills on Saturdays
with junior partners dressed up in rags,
who shimmy seedlings from plastic trays;
trowel loose dirt from grocery bags;

while speaking to one another, in
the clipped tones of the billable.
Brushing the green dirt from their skin,
they carry home their basketsful

of corn and squash; and, tracking through
gold lobbies to an upper floor,
adjust a green shade on a view
in which their plot's a pocket square.

At midday, from our plot, wild grass
bleeds odor as the sunlight dries
condoms and wrappers, whose ambergris
stutters a colonnade of flies.

At day's end, the towers draw
the last light to their window vents;
deadening the parkway's roar
like tombs, inlaid with smoke. And, once

we pack, and stand, the live, black shade
trebling off embankment walls
breeds moths, that, wind-tumbled, abrade
their likenesses to horses' skulls;

as scum chops down a pebbled grade
and seethes on a splash stone green with moss.

The Green Banks of the River

Directionless, on foot, you at last reach the river's edge
where your eyes flock to the arc lamps on a bridge.
Their neon, bunched like church bells, roils the water
as a tine struck on a glass damps the laughter

rolled in the wake of a sundowner upstream.
Close in, the current, picked out by a beam,
quickens where a shallow stone
tears white devices in the froth, and a bedouin

crab darts over packed sand. As, over the rails,
the boat's reflection on the busy swells
haloes the couples waiting on the deck,
who, glancing at each other when they speak,

speak volumes to the drift-wreck. In a black vest,
the best man lifts an iced flute in a toast
to the flushed pair whose table heads the aisle—
here the boat slips from the sightline of your trail

as applause falls like the slur of a silver chain.
Whatever lifted you from your routine
and left you scrabbling through a cement ditch;
weed stung; trying to intuit which

of the fading paths will see you to your car
trembles, divided, with the watery star
shining stateless in the waves, where, sped
by the lit boat, it plays out crooked thread.

To those still on the deck this time of night,
those out walking the river with handheld lights
signal wildly, as, nearing the river's mouth,
they throw their arms up on the suddenly steep path.

Eden

Radical girl; shy daughter of a teacher;
so beautiful she stopped the cleat of shadow on
the sun dial. Lithe, proportioned by that god
who packs quick rage in beasts—I couldn't reach her,
the bouncing betties on her halter top
not for a self-declared bohemian

and she, hall-mirrored, knew it. Cruelty, love,
were joined by her in a long-handled scythe
that stacked male Ids like wheat, the tangled bales
and mowers mindless of the blood stalked in their path
a smear of jealousy for those who looked on, nails
bit to the quick; obsessive; seeking proof.

Promiscuous, the rumors reached her father—
collector of rare firsts, curries, and jazz—
who, having named her for a paradise
now watched her work grown men into a lather
and date the ones with money and big cars;
get high successive nights in different bars.

Trapped in the slow round of an ingénue,
she'd wave as I rocked a planter for a key
then lie back in the dapple off a pool . . .
taut, tremoring midsection streaked with oil;
tipped-back head; and sun-flocked hair aglow
with an experience not had for free.

What conversation could I have with her?
I couldn't speak from the deep part of hope
that saw her as a balm, one I'd use to dress
an ego burnished with aggressiveness.
Like Jack LaLanne, I'd shadow box, skip rope,
and deck the linebacker who grabbed her hair.

Who was she? Twirling like a barber's pole,
her vanities changed place with qualities
both shy and whole. My first experience
of separation from a shared ideal,
the breeze that raised her towel off the fence
and broke my thin composure by the trees

still comes to mind, heavy with sweat and oil.
Some night we'd catch a movie, then, on the walk home,
decide to take the long way through the park.
Where we could talk, and through the push and pull
light a connection tight as a chromosome
and cup our hands—together—round that spark.

Library of Alexandria

A retired teacher says, with no little regret,
his library's been picked apart by wolves;
ex-students, who, at his instruction, caught
his passion for the books lined on his shelves.

His library in the telling's a living thing,
patched with an inlet's colors over many years,
with this blue heron of a novel; that red-wing
blackbird spreading wing against its own reverse.

If it's a living thing, then let it thrive
scattered across his margin of the continent
in the fat tracts where his ex-students live
still lean, still sniffing out a book's intent.

In one of those lost copies, an inscribed verse
pans that impromptu signing's flashing course.

The Short Drive Home

1

It's with me still: the screened-in porch, cane chairs, iced tea
sweating in thick-seamed tumblers; you reading from your novel as
wind slips in the fresh wake of a prop plane overhead.

I watch its tail light shift from red, to blue, to green
and hear a car gun down the dark, faux-marble road.
This turns you to the boy who crashed the week before

on the loose slip of gravel below Friant Dam.
It was his choice, you say; if he'd installed a roll-bar
he could have walked away; but foolish, young, aching

to be reborn he chose to die. Your novel scrapes
dead wax from a tablet, and buzzes with slant views
of night skies knit from ours; red-shifted galaxies

rifted of their precisions by ruffling solar winds.
With a conviction half that of a convert, half
that of a bore who won't allow a game to end

you say you dreamed the shadow of your own past lives—
whose pressure racked a typeface changeable as cloud—
when you began the book you read from now. I nod,

taken as always by your tough humility;
and simply won't acknowledge that your crazy talk
proves your illness has won; that the circle of past life

you endlessly elaborate with a few friends
is your refusal to acknowledge your own death
which nears, and seeks a token, for the gates of horn.

2

It was the 70s, when other worlds—each cast
like haloed afterimages from ours—sailed out
on a bright sea of diminishing returns; screens lit

in the suburban malls with anime cartoons
that siphoned peril, as lithe blond protagonists
flipped through a stack of violent possibilities

and scorned, like genre, to leave any one behind.
Just *why*—glassed-in affluence smutched by the burnt cork
of '68; each cause still drum-and-fifing toward

a bright slope on a hill; the front's acidic fire
eating into the structures of rhetoric
as through a warehouse of machinery: gears locked

and fluttering with the power of unusable
weapons; silos spitting fire in the wastes of fields;
oceans netted by the thrusts and counterthrusts

of cloaked subs, racked with missiles, deep beneath green waves;
so many people stoned, or sealed in glass frames;
such brittleness and excess paired in art and life—

slow down, I hear you say, before you paint such broad,
bright strokes; *backdrop* is a critic's term, and means,
quite literally, a dirty cloth; much better to observe

spires on a shadowed hill; or the demon sprites of alcohol
spiraling the conversation in a crowd, than twist
such party-favors out of crumpled strips of news.

3

I wonder lately why that chain of nights—gemmed glass,
red nicks where the cane chair cut my legs—have corkscrewed
so far back in memory that what seem several lives

have come and gone since then; and why, each time one passed,
I brought so little of my past life to the next:
each circle of new friends never quite aligning with

the old, and always fewer friends in each new town.
Bad faith, you said, about a minor character
will kill the reader's faith in the protagonist.

You offered so much sweet advice those nights; were you—
I think this now, a world away—somehow afraid?
Truth was, I didn't listen; driving home, I shook my head

at the grand, synoptic wanderings of your novel; its world
that bent so easily to show a chain of worlds
like two mirrors tilted to infinity by

a bored child on a Sunday afternoon;
or like that "gold to aery thinness beat,"
that pivoted, pure metaphor, in my weak grasp of love.

4

When I recall those nights—my body as it was;
blanched moon, low houses hoarding coils of light—
I don't remember any of your novel's plot;

but with those evenings I reclaim your augur's voice;
insecticide-doused netting swelled with the wind
and, just out of earshot, Quaalude-glittered moans

from the bored nymphs and satyrs lying back with such
sublime, if selfish, confidence in this one life.
One life; your voice rustling off dot-matrix sheets; wind

steady in the fine netting belled onto the porch.
How strong you were—and if I didn't recognize
your strength as such; if my judgment of your novel crossed

belief in poetry with less experience;
I didn't grasp what you were facing then: dreams of
a snapped hoop bounding down a hillside toward a canyon,

whose sun-whipped precincts, red as Zion, bled iron dust
when, at day's end, red light tipped haphazard glass
on the foreshortened strata on the cliffs, and clouds

on the marbled endpapers of your father's books—
Dickens, Trollope, Thackeray, Sir Walter Scott.
Whose country towns lay hip to shoulder with your plains;

their chapel lanes thinned to a beer-blond light in which
old men argued ten-pins in a gravel pitch, or a June
storm rumbled the staunch roof beams of your parent's house.

5

At their age, you sailed the world in a fiberglass boat;
bottle-nosed dolphins, you wrote, knifing alongside night
after day, leering in the spray, towing the hemispheres

toward strange new skies, as you tapped the sparking shortwave
for storm news or cabin mates' voices, raw as the gulls'.
When I hope now that the failures of my company

did not cast you adrift; that my close-held ambition
complemented yours; it then occurs to me—too late;
abidingly real—you never needed my belief,

perhaps anyone's. Only now, when the harm frayed
from everything I haven't done anticipates
the coming centuries, whose caul and tar will pitch

my soul against the confines of a small black box
of sleep—bodiless sleep dreamt at fever's rate—
can I appreciate the strength with which you read

your novel with your bright, scuffed voice; and laughed when I
stifled a yawn so fiercely my whole body shook; and slipped
ten dollars in my pocket for the short drive home.

The Rose Farm

Black oaks nod in a wind rolled off the fens.
Stage-whispering shadows, churches dot the fields.
    Sunlight, leapt from a puddle, gilds
the dented flashing on a shed roof, tense

and cutting where a swift scats round a post.
Angling west, we take the paths churned between
    scots pine, fir, burnt cedar; all green
and gelid as a coin stopped up with frost.

Light hurries over bright facsimiles
of rape fields, burred with wind. Free-swinging bells
    hammer scalding, wind-borne peals
that make the wall-eyed gargoyles hug their knees

more tightly, as clouds stem the humped yard's brink
of shade, quarried stone, frayed grass. Opacities
    catch as the red kites from the glass
and stammer ravines the saints cross on a plank.

We skirt a graveyard where a banker's vault
breathes a damp chill on the lawn. Someone's crept
    past the slung chain into the crypt;
a beer can rusts a coarse flame, red with malt.

If we slow, or break stride, our distances
bunch like fistfuls of satin in our wake.
    Balance; take my hand; now, for our sake,
these paths will dead end on thick trellises

of rose, and we'll sling baskets at our sides;
bosomy mats worn black by the clipped buds.
    Broad noon. The sun lights, in dry beds,
damp, acidic reds; and, at its full height, rides

no higher than the roofs at the field's edge.
Torn petals smudge the red crown on our pledge.

III

Three-Card Monte

Despite the worlds it spins off every day;
    the million worlds that branch out from changed plans;

coins tossed in fountains; unread letters; play
    of numbers in a bookie's notebook; chance

always casts its influence in a bronze
    many-sided as a dealer palming a queen;

the Spanish Armada, broken by high winds,
    granting the fire ships their pretty screen.

With lantern-jawed Nevada, chance affirms
    our difficulty with accepting just

one life, that, through an actuary's terms,
    inscribes a book-lined apartment with the dust

of a great reckoning: nothing will change.
    Or, in Vegas, everything, if we allow

flash pyramids their shrill uses of the orange
    corrosions heaped at day's end on a scow.

So too the tanned, white-haired receptionist
    who, sitting beneath a trademark, counseling many,

    sighed as she haloed a quick pick with a penny:
"If I get this, you won't see me for dust."

Next

The moon, a flint struck off the Capitol's
lit dome, weighs daybreak at a border fence
whose gaps, to those still waiting, seethe like shoals.
Fresh off the Hill, new heads of state announce
successes, to the click of the capped heels
on the boots of the guard at the tomb of the unknowns,
who processes, turns, and tucks his rifle butt
hard against his shoulder, as his free hand cuts

a nerveless arc. At dawn, the host dictates
a memo to the southern hemisphere
about the orbital decay of a tin star
that, skipped white off the atmosphere, dilates
the guards' attention at a checkpoint, bright
with floodlight where a family sinks to its knees.
A ruined base camp mines his emphases.
Done, he walks a garden walled with light.

Joints frost in lockers near the docks, where cranes,
pivoting, swing containers down from ships
that change their provenance with each new sky.
In the far ports, gulls drop from riggings dense
as tariff stamps, then glide past fouled hulls
as guards stamp in the warehouse doors. Come night,
forgotten culverts sweat where hostages
tremble in cut light as the stepped-up guards

play flashlights over the razor-wired vents.
In the green zone, a statue, brusque as chain,
calls down a wind on gumwrappers and wire.
Its grimace at the host of cinderblocks
recalls the corpses, blindfolded in pits, whose night
bristles the rooftop antennas with rage.
Which bucks our F-14s, as their instruments
whirl toward a lit deck, burst hard through a black wave.

Immigrant Song

An anthem from the wild half of my youth—
the singer wailing triads just off key;
fuzzed guitar, slurred bass, repeating high hat brusque
as Vikings who dragged a long boat from the sea
to a perch high on the shore; the prow's red eyes

vacant as they slung piglets onto the deck
to bleed out in the cockroaches and furs.
Though they'd never play a town as small as ours,
the white noise stripping their accents of their lilt
brought their stateless English home to us

in a valley English hadn't ruled for long.
Moveable feasts, our parties quieted when Jimmy
picked out a solo on the higher frets;
scattershot triplets a trampoline off which
naked girls cavorted to a lash

of music; lithe goads for the garage bands
who bore the standard on their Saturdays
with lunges toward the beat; choked wheeze and cough
of a flank shot rhino charging the hunter's gun:
thick legs stumping like pistons; ungainly,

turreted body too broad and low to slow
or turn, yet gathering a whip-shot speed
that was snuffed out as the cartridge jumped; amps
blowing the penny fuses yet again;
afterechoes sawdust in the rafters.

If I attended one, it seemed a thousand
weekend parties, just why a mystery.
I knew I disliked the threat of violence
so many of the others seemed to love;
denim-clad bikers bursting into song

raucously, pitching each other into walls;
their Jack Daniels or Budweiser sloshed loose
in violent little rills. If I ducked, or
pushed back, cornered, I couldn't let fear daub
a fresh twitch at the corner of my mouth, so glared . . .

My friends and I would be there for some girl
who, in a first flush of adolescent heat, had
bared a midriff, or shyly dropped a gaze;
swiveling our attention. By the time we showed,
the same, now jaded girl would be hemmed in by

protectors, brash in their ownership, with a rough
sun of hammered bronze, or a gold roach clip
dangling from a thong around her neck—
possession now a prior, close-held pact
disorienting as the keg or bong.

The dust bowl spiked their manner; what shaped mine?
Was I the immigrant, who, darker skinned,
wants to possess what he knows he cannot; pluck
some brass ring from a honeybaited trap?
But, no; that's too dramatic; I didn't see

myself as such; that status more a crease
in the compacted warp of those hot nights;
our old-world portraits doused with shade at home.
At some pink stucco house on the town's edge
set among fig groves that channeled a wind

warm as the ashes tipped from the smudge pots
we drove up, snuffed the lights, and pushed ourselves
through the front door on the slightest invitation—
rooms smoke-filled, lights turned low, pickings meager—
and still I smiled, and ducked my height; too eager.

Two Sticks and a Cake

The shock sped by the planes' refusal of
miniature sheared that morning into halves:
a present, choked with ash; and past, whose chaff
skirted the task force as it plowed the waves

and fought down goat paths with armed clans. Our affluence
threatened, charges streamed like filings between poles;
that our fathers had bred this hatred in silk tents;
that new sheikhs fanned resentments in the coals

burning in storefront braziers. And flags appeared,
it seemed in nervousness, on full-page spreads,
rear windows, overpasses; as we all steered
for rockbound harbors grapeshot with autumn reds

where cheering crowds ducked to a megaphone. Till shock grew deft
and we forgot we hadn't known: the stars go on the left.

Peterborough

    What's in a name starts with a place,
a much fought-over place, where dead-sea corals
        collect and leaf
    and stars bank in a reef
in shadow, on a damp stone wall; say, in Peterborough.

    What's in a name runs from a place
through pawn shops ribboned like a quarry. Swallow-
        stained passages
    buff hope from languages
that bring their speakers just so far, in Peterborough.

    What's in a name renews a place
in ballads quarreled stem and root by scholars.
        Bald journeymen
    still start their shifts at dawn
and lay snares in the shine of night, in Peterborough;

    then, tossing back a bitter, place
wet crowns on the ruff of Elvis Presley.
        Hard bread and cheese
    cue tourist pleasantries
and swiped cards glint with firelight, in Peterborough.

    To shunt a name back to its source
wheel the mirrored trolley out of shadow.
        In its reverse
    a void painted with stars
nubs embolisms with grotesques. In Peterborough,

a gray slab with a comet's face
shutters the king's first wife, whose rawboned carol
            will long outlast
      this pile. As we file past,
our thoughts catch in the wild stars of the cathedral;

wheel in place of the painted gold stars in the ceiling at
   Peterborough.

Thirst

1

25, and with my lover in
Manhattan for a brief stay; heat and grime
fluttering the soiled pennants of mid-July
and islanding the rooftops where we drank,
as guests; her sister both our guide and host.
On our first day, we heard the latest from
the harried Village clinic where she interned;
even met, late that same day, in a red-leather
receiving room midtown, her latest love;
an orthopedic surgeon with a trained
stammer of exhaustion in his hand and eye.
Next day, while sitting in a street café,
we saw him walking by. Appearing out
of nowhere from the crowd's blue dyes, bare skin, broad heat
he seemed embarrassed; bowed away quickly, when

we waved him to a stop beside our chairs.
That night, her sister asked repeatedly
what had he been wearing, and tapped her brow
trying to recall the clothes he'd worn
the day before; her interest tunneling
from pique, toward jealousy or love, until
we left her for a club's hot, crowded floor;
the silk rope at the entrance parting on
abandons pitched in sequins from the lights.
Sweat drenched, we stumbled back at four a.m.
and bucked our twin-sized bed across the room;
then slept, legs twined, till one; then drove that night
to a friend's shack on the Long Island shore.
And woke in the starved belly of the roar.

2

That afternoon, we'd browsed the Village shops'
ankhs, prisms, cameos, veronicas;
objects whose possession—prinked with tissue;
recessed in blue glare—somehow reversed poles
and, coarse as trinkets raided from a tomb,
arced as we considered them through flawed glass.
In one bright case, face cards with lash-thin mouths
dabbed with a mosquito's wing of kohl
replayed the terror of a minor, much-reproduced
king, who saw nothing, eyes sewn in his robes;
wormholes seething in the roof and floor.
A few shops had the bright, x-rated cards
whose penetrations, lit like a convenience store
at midnight, flashed where, years before, panels
of riverlight plashed red motto, blue guitar.

Headlines scrolled in black on white marquees;
rusted tackle on the fire escapes
backlit by neon gels. Hot air quickened the wet
brush slap of a tank top on a sweating girl
who scowled, then skipped downstairs toward a train
cowled in burnt oil. What trees there were
were cut with shade; what light shone off the wet
skin flashing in the bars. We drove the lit
expressway with that tumult at our backs,
and arriving at that shack on a black shore
walked the empty dunes as if still in Times Square—
eyes turned up; stars like cinder-fed smoke
close overhead; drift and plunge of noise
scouring our minds of everything but
love, and pitching forward, racked with salt.

3

In the hashed blocks of newsprint, HIV
was a newly diagnosable condition;
rattle of night sweats a first tremor of death;
the news almost a temperance tract against
a night spent with a stranger; thin gay men
so marked by death that people feared their tears.
Rumors flew like streamers from the wards
of Brooklyn Heights or St. Vincent's: that drugs
were useless; that the crazed morbidity
put even doctors in mind of the Black Death;
that whole streets and apartment blocks were thick
with dying, silence in a young man's rooms
meaning he was likely to have killed himself;
that even the ash from crematoria
was dangerous, and better scattered over water

than on land; that biting flies and (she shuddered)
mosquitoes could transmit fresh virus; that
we all were living on the thinnest ledge.
The doctors seemed in full retreat; the city
frightened and astonished by the baths
and what appeared a death dance of young men.
That day, we picked our way among the shops,
the wet heat of the city a swung crop.
Gun metal gray on gray, the mid-town scrims
billowed and touched the bare-skinned limbs of models
with opacity at the slightest luff of breeze.
On the D train, we turned at a tunnel's mouth
to follow the scroll of a kinetic Keith Haring
tableau: lumpen marionettes shouting
in black stars through the margins of new graves.

4

In the first flush of a more prosaic
illness; in the high Sierra near a stream
of melted snow; in the rifted blue light
of early spring, which, at that height, was spring's
only as winter pleased. Wide, quick current
braiding the switchbacked narrows of tumbled stone;
heaped-up edgings stitching endlessly
in weedy vernicles of white and green;
blunted wraps of snow on the mid-stream rocks
catching the echoes breaking down the water.
A brackish taint at the back of my throat, I leant
forward, crouching with my hands spread on a slick
green stone; and drank, lightheaded, from a rill;
then settled back in that brittle, white pine
amphitheater, thirstier than before.

The Bar

The gossip shifted to a friend of ours
who, in the lean weeks before his bar exam,

woke in a strange beach house in the wee hours
as the blond vagrants who'd invited him

stripped and made mouths for a photographer
in a clinch modeled for a magazine.

No fool, our friend. Back to a sun-blistered door,
he rummaged through a bag dropped in the sheen

of a driftwood fire, then faced the camera
wearing a horned mask. And, with that choice,

protected his career; free to marry the
heat snapping off bright wood, to the raw voice

of someone crying in the dunes out back.
Rolled on the waves, the sparkling pediment

of a full moon tipping white light down its track
cross-cut that rage till the shine of its intent

tumbled heedlessly down paths of glinting spar.
Edged by the roar, a small band swam out later

through the fierce draw to a white-bottomed sand bar,
where they waded the quicksilver green water

as maidenhaired breakers curled from a deep
that cancelled any thought. If those who dreamed

of a perpetual resort, and those whose lack of sleep
was a tin roof to their ambition, seemed

equal, on that bar; well, they'd never meet again,
unless in court; nor bother to look back

on a road flushed white with dawn. Hid by a dune,
the host no one remembered kneeled to a cracked

stone, and snugged the house key back in its hollow;
in a bed near a seaside door, as a weekday squatter

rushed out, eyes down, to a car banked in shadow;
and the view dissembled in blue panes over the water.

Rule

The hubs of systems branch relationship
through transepts, royal in red passages,
to vaults, whose keystones bridge their ruin with
concurrency, in bands that swell like moons.

The engineers who inked such diagrams
were themselves drawn by fugues braided like smoke
ribboning off a missile, or states collapsed
in gaudy simultaneity to a goat's foot

of ash. Fashion twists their hierarchies
into scarabs of black wire that gnaw the hills,
yet still wins the attention of the millions
hunched before their sets, where massacres,

stalled conferences, cop shows quiver like lace.
Engineers, like artists, card relationship
through syllable and circuit board; oil paint
and centrifuge; scattering infinities that trip

our voices down a trilling optical fiber.
Their portrait gallery is dark and close;
consider the queen's anesthetist, John Snow,
who diagrammed a cholera outbreak

on a street map of the stricken neighborhood,
then noticed how the fatal incidents
clustered round a well—worn path and signpost;
causality appearing then like grace;

blunt lines of relationship snapping in place
as the council, removing the handle, then released
millions from the illness. The well's brick hold,
mossed with sewage, trapped a thousand voices

in the flat disk at bottom capped with night.
Ringed by the drays jostling past the well,
those waters, tasted now by just the moss,
were cheated of those deaths, and sullenly ebbed

to the quaking tide flats of the shit gray Thames.
Though our nostalgia for the deficits
of ignorance remains, on late winter Sundays
when hours stamp mirrors with black, petaling silvers

which spread through the low-walled
gardens of our sleep, through an air thick
as pyrite rolled in lesions on a meteor,
then blossom in the cities ribboned with faults:

Tyre, Warsaw, Prague. In John Snow's London—
adulterated flour; thick bands of bell-rung smoke—
the thousand deaths deferred in that neighborhood
returned to their heavy singularity:

solitaries walking home; couples
decked in ostrich plumes and scraped calf skin
taking the dance floor in branched candlelight
where they bowed, and spun, their patterns anchored by

the women's cleavage, and the wet splurge of wax.
One woman who had moved before the outbreak
to the green slip of a Hampstead garden lane
still died, because she'd had her water shipped

from the contaminated Broad Street well,
having grown accustomed to its taste—pall
of habit balancing Snow's diagram
with the inked spot of the outlier, whose death

took wing. Crossed by the green light in her new home
the chop of filthy water in a jug
still quickens with the faces of the neighbors
who once neared; bent; and, drinking, turned away.

IV

Smell of the Lamp

As when, working, I feel the blue plat
of sleep edge open, ridging my mind—
no matter how hard I strain, how fierce
my will to concentrate, exhaustion
bids me drop my head, close my eyes, bide
the pliant shadowforms' cartwheeling play.
So I will doze some little time; skirt
sleep's blue interior; then wake, flush
with readiness, my mind alert, fixed
on a cave wall where scatting ovals
of light rouse stick herds to flight again;
heraldic flank and hoof; ash-violent stars.

    My mind now swallow-tailed with concentration;
everything suffused with harsh white light.

Reunion

Thumbing a silvered yearbook, I note the twinned
sentiment and rage, buff as the graces,
posed with my class, whose cheer, fresh off the stand,
petals in the soft focus round their faces.

Denial, edged with pride, ovals the few
whose grants now rope artisans into the naves
where dead-eyed north winds, hooped in filthy straw,
exhort a copper-green flood. Restored, those waves

tumble the outskirts of a northern city
where freedmen cut copper wing-struts in their stalls.
Unfinished, their expressions, and more's the pity;
the flood tide, as it nears, upends the walls

gone hollow in a light rayed from a kiln.
The fountains of the great deep crack and void
whirlpools that swallow all thought of cloud or sun.
Bare-shouldered angels jostle and sink, wild-eyed.

Sol

1

. . . or lifelight, whose hooded path through the dry trees
powders moss-smut and bark as I walk by,
all of us: poplar, ash, white chute of cloud
remark your passing and turn after you
unconsciously, with lowered eyes or leaves, assays

of word or mist, that fix you in a rush-mat sky.
Bright canter, whose plumes arc loads of static
in every live receiving dish; bored traveler,
whose molt of hydrogen and carbon plumbs
wastes light takes millennia to cross; cave dweller,

whose actions slip, too absolute for thought,
a whole niche from the periodic table,
dusting nickel with a froth of platinum.
The plumes recorded by our satellites
charge in the wind that stirs your gravid lakes

of helium, whipping dust spouts and vortices
that curl, and billow, carded with black spots.
Torn grass and cloud defray your stack of heat
and scatter it like straw, leaving you at day's end
roaring outside the safe house of our sleep.

2

I note you like a pendant on the roofs
when I go out at noon, and watch you trawl heaped stones
for bits of quartz and mica; the whole exchange
a catalog of light by light. I watch your trees
expressing their confinement in your wind;

silversided leaves; chimneysoot branches.
When you lean in and thumb my eyes, I think
of the condemned in Dante's hell, who greet
the pilgrim with the phrase: 'O you, who see the sun.'
The patched white oak bears offerings, that, stacked

on your first planet's hammered tray, are less
than ash. Oceans hide their depths from you
but even at their lowest weep clots of ore.
If you take notice, I am scalded, and,
shivering, sulk indoors for days, till I hear

your emissaries sharp in the first light
and watch you garland junk-filled lots, tendering
columns white as the Forum's pitch of ash,
and hear you cast a high, blank wind whose voice
biases the rain and draws your charging storms.

3

The plum tree, lit by you, shakes silken reds
in cymbal-dashed patterns like Solomon's wives,
tenting the front rooms of even those thugs
who, lit by a desire that drags through violence,
confuse approval with a child's smudged face.

I con that red tree for its lesson, but
find nothing, only anger. Meanwhile, you stir
shadows with a rib of moon, in alleys where
our dead and their tormenters meet, through a membrane
of fear. Moon that trenches dunes with hoops of wind;

agitating crystals locked in stone
till they shine like cities from your height, and you bank
and carry your strict fire underground
with—for reasons never clear—a thread of flesh.
So at some far date our world might reappear

under changed skies—manic, lashing, coiled—
and feel your light, now thinned and reddened,
carol untrammeled off plateau or wave
and fold the rusts that once were coins in clay
as you collapse, and swell, and swallow your nearest

fire scuffed planets, eye on a black hole's grave.

Georgetown

On a July midday, a thunderstorm
blacked the midtown sky, and, large-grained, swelled with light,
made a Roman audience of the trees.
                              Crimps of white lightning
unstitched the opal hammock of the clouds
and heat bled from the asphalt in damp gouts
as the walkers, hunching forward,
peg-legged to the doorways, where the vents
of water faded quickly from their clothes.

So many of the walkers were young women
in pressed silk skirts and strapless tops
who, when sheltered, raised their arms
to recompose their hair, cheeks flushed
with effort and displeasure as they twisted
first toward each other, then the crowd
surging behind them on the walk. Unbonneted
one combed her fingers through her hair;

rolled it in a still damp sheaf;
and, finishing, turned to hail a cab,
but found none there. Visibly
upset, she seemed to catalog
her options: run back to the store,
or stay and watch the storm . . . the rain
fell heavier, curtaining
the door in which she stood, half poised

for flight, half settled in to waste
a good part of the afternoon.
The lightning made her cell phone risky.
No one would miss her for an hour.
The peaked waves in the downpour struck
the steep roofs with such warmth, mist
collected in the overhanging trees.   Come
night, how cold and wet she'd be.

The Black Oak in the Storm

One Thursday night, a storm unrolled and shook
black cloud over embassy row. A white shaft,
more terrible for its ribboning drift,
echoed and struck a hundred-year black oak

whose singed crown fell across a power line.
Blue insulators fused, as the bolt drowned
particles conducted off the wind
in the steel outcrops of a waste lot. When

it struck, the bolt howled a like shape from the tree,
which then spat out that lambency, icily
netting stirrups of steel. In the wet heat,

the century's black oak lay on its side,
greenly dying; live stanchions arced; and the wind shied
crisps of halo from the lines downed in the street.

The Parkway

1

St. Valentine, herald of dusty roses, had had
his day, another bound in cinched red foil
and puckered crimson doilies; the young and not-so-young
buying flowers, broiling steaks, making love;
so much it seemed the sky would flush with it;
so many smothered come cries denting the clouds.
The keen note of the solitaries struck
as well; the damaged and awkward; indolent
or curt; for whom the evening fixed a beam
on the clean cloth, and brightly polished silver,
of a fresh-set table.
     Late from work,
I'd eased my car onto the parkway ramp,
and as I waited for the light to change
the woman in the car in front of mine
jumped out, and, skipping toward the car behind me
held up her phone, pointed to herself, and mouthed
you called for me?
     The man behind the wheel
nodded at once, and, certain now, she sashayed
back to her car, and, as the light turned green,
accelerated up the ramp.
     I couldn't help but watch
their intimate, conspiratorial weave
along the lanes, and, stopped at the next light, saw
her downturned face cupped in the sideview's glass,
clawed by ease . . .

                        she smoked, eyes unfocused, stirred
by neither fear nor pique; the plucked set of her brow
and smooth cut of her mouth more beautiful
for seeming caught. As the light changed, she shifted
powerfully, pushing her shoulder over the wheel
of her battered, wine-colored import; then turned
into a motel parking lot. He slowed,
and turned, and in the low green light the bared
flesh of her midriff flashed as she stood from her car;
the tableau gone in the instant I drove by.

2

Of course, what did I know; what good is it
remembering a dance so intimate
the parkway blushed at daybreak? As the maid
yanked clean linens off the shelves, those two
were nowhere to be found; cars banked to the curbs
of different satellite neighborhoods.
                                              So long,
old prince; all eagerness and quarrelsome haste;
you'll stand from that stranger's body soon enough
and take your place amid the hawks and doves
strutting at the craps table; shoulders hunched
in the moment before the four and three
wink manic on green felt. You'll take your place
and slip your date's black gown straps from her shoulders;
your losses on the bright map of the table
confetti on the grand stair to your room.
You'll take your place, yet still grow bored, until
you prowl the parkway again with your cell phone;
scanning the turnoffs till you have to call
the escort service, to ask for a girl whose looks
remind you of a star; and seek her out
on a parkway named for a confederate general.

Goodbye, brave escort; kept by the chirring phone
from the hard round of the streetwalker; your life
spiraling through indecision until
you found yourself these means. *And what that means,*
you said, *is that I have some regulars*
who call when they don't want to be alone;
as if I were a therapist—to no one;
to your memory of your parents. And the cash,
never enough, was a necessity;
your days off washed with Dr. Phil's slack chorus.

*You have to pay attention when they first
set eyes on you—do they meet or drop your eyes?
Before, it's like some salt's
been rubbed in theirs—they shake and stare. After,
whether in a car, or in a room,
you'd better get your things and just get out—
their guilt can make them cry, and, when they cry,
they can hit you.*

3

                  Your car needs work; misses
and coughs furred oil onto your parking space.
The cherry trees still clot your eyes with red
as you drive the sheltered parkway, level and free,
and glimpse the white interiors of town cars
whose matrons knock back antihistamines
that wash their eyes of trouble, while the low sun
tears red pigment from the leaves.
                                    When you stand
from your wine-colored car, whether to buy
a bag of groceries, or meet a man
in the wind-scalloped shell of another parking lot,
you'll prop thin panels of the news against
the hard tack of the parkway, and leave
some shadow of that other world intact;
one you'd deny to anyone who asked;
a world in which your long view of the parkway
folds into the mountain views of home.
You see your face, made up, racked by a love,
reflected in the long reflecting pools
that skip your thoughts at midday past the script
that played the night before.
                                  Compass moon
and dash; black needle on the speedometer
quivering over the sun-cracked numerals
as you bank, slow, then pick up useless speed
along the parkway, whose pines and hillocks fold
effortlessly behind the flesh-pink monuments.

4

When, pausing in the stale air of the hall,
you turn the key, then step into your rooms,
the close air blocks your mind until you drop
the day's mail on a sofa filled with mail.
And in the world the catalogs reveal,
rainbows pour their declensions on the malls
where children yank ensembles off the racks
and, smoothing a sleeve along one arm, dance
the body over themselves in a slant bay
of mirrors.   Deviated crowd slipping
from the bright foils, they cast themselves in its hollows
and, tricked out in their new clothes, nod, and stir
attention like a fine shower across a lake.
For a promotion, or a holiday,
a chain has set bright glow sticks in white urns.
Picked up, their rainbows vein the crowd as it flows
down the main aisle, vaulted by noise, and trapped
sparrows flaying papery shadow for seed.
With the reed-thin lights, children race ahead,
drawn by the shop terraces; their sneakers
chirping as they halt pell-mell on the tile
before the screeching tombs of an arcade.
As their parents slow before a blue placard
of a cruise ship anchored in a white harbor
and, draped with confetti, clawed by red noise,
vie for a portside stateroom cold as a dream.

Song

Now of an age when time is everything,
we wake in the first light to slate gray birds.
      Sweeping in view
off shrouded trees, they peck and choke down curds
of suet; scold the menacing shadow; sing.

Honeycombed with song, our summer drags
ivy like barbed wire through the watershed,
      where, in stained pews,
saprophytic fungi ridge and spread
wrinkled ears to the snap of plastic bags.

Last spring, we slept with the window open
listening to the blackbird's voluble plea;
      and when our love came due
we heard within our words the window tree:
dragged by the weight of the moon, thick-leaved, misshapen.

Notes and Dedications

"The Short Drive Home," part 3, quotes a famous line from John Donne's "A Valediction: forbidding Mourning."

"Peterborough"—Catherine of Aragon, Henry VIII's first wife, is buried in Peterborough Cathedral.

"Thirst," part 3—in the early 1980s, the artist Keith Haring drew on blank advertising panels in New York City subway stations.

"Rule" gleans historical detail and analysis from Judith Summers, *Soho: A History of London's Most Colourful Neighborhood* (Bloomsbury, 1989), and Steven Johnson, *The Ghost Map: The Story of London's Most Terrifying Epidemic* (Riverhead, 2006).

"Georgetown" steals a phrase from David St. John's "Elegy," in *The Shore* (Houghton Mifflin, 1980).

"Food Lion, Winchester, Tennessee" is dedicated to Wyatt Prunty and Cherie Bedell Peters.

"Wildest Hour" is dedicated to Doug Macomber.

"Library of Alexandria" is dedicated to Bob Jarnagin.

"Peterborough" is dedicated to Chantal Armstrong.

"The Rose Farm" and "Song" are dedicated to Alison Paddock.

Acknowledgments

Grateful acknowledgement to the editors and publishers of the following, where these poems appeared, sometimes in earlier versions:

The Missouri Review Online: "Eden"

Ploughshares: "The Riverboat" (as "Luck," vol. 25:1)

Sewanee Theological Review: "Georgetown" (vol. 47:2)

Slate™ Magazine (www.slate.com): "Food Lion, Winchester, Tennessee"

The Yale Review: "The Rose Farm" (vol. 95:4)

The Swallow Anthology of New American Poets: "The Aughts," "Food Lion, Winchester, Tennessee," "Next," "Song," and "Three-Card Monte"

Deep thanks to the University of the South for a Tennessee Williams fellowship which helped me work on these poems, and for the self-same fellowship and excellence of their community;

To Alan Shapiro, for his comments on an earlier version of the manuscript;

To Bob Jarnagin, who read many of these poems in draft, and whose pitch-perfect observations were in themselves the best form of encouragement;

To Chard DeNiord for selecting the book, and to Tayve Neese and Terry Lucas for their many apt suggestions, and for bringing the book to the light of day;

And, finally, to Alison, whose support and patience made this work possible, and whose love, lit with too many insights to name, threw the world into such high relief.

About the Author

Joe Osterhaus is the author of two previous collections: *The Domed Road*, in *Take Three: AGNI New Poets Series: 1*; and *Radiance*. He was a scholar at Bread Loaf and a Walter E. Dakin Fellow at the Sewanee Writers' Conference, and has taught at Boston University, University College at Washington University, and the Krieger School of Arts and Sciences at Johns Hopkins. He was also Tennessee Williams Fellow and Visiting Lecturer at the University of the South. His work has appeared in such journals as *AGNI, BOMB, The Formalist, Harvard Review, The Nebraska Review, The Paris Review, Ploughshares, Poetry Daily, Slate, Triquarterly,* and *The Yale Review,* and in such anthologies as *American Poetry: The Next Generation; The New American Poets: A Bread Loaf Anthology;* and *The Swallow Anthology of New American Poets*. He lives with his wife and son in Northern Virginia, where he works in IT services.

About the Book

The Short Drive Home was designed at Trio House Press through the collaboration of:

Terry Lucas, Lead Editor
Tayve Neese, Supporting Editor
Cover Photo: Berenice Abbott, "George Washington Bridge, New York,"
Cover Photo Digital image courtesy of the Getty's Open Content Program.
Dorinda Wegener, Cover Design
Lea Deschenes, Interior Design

The text is set in Adobe Caslon Pro.

The publication of this book is made possible, whole or in part, by the generous support of the following individuals and/or agencies:

Anonymous

About the Press

Trio House Press is a collective press. Individuals within our organization come together and are motivated by the primary shared goal of publishing distinct American voices in poetry. All THP published poets must agree to serve as Collective Members of the Trio House Press for twenty-four months after publication in order to assist with the press and bring more Trio books into print. Award winners and published poets must serve on one of four committees: Production and Design, Distribution and Sales, Educational Development, or Fundraising and Marketing. Our Collective Members reside in cities from New York to San Francisco.

Trio House Press adheres to and supports all ethical standards and guidelines outlined by the CLMP.

The Editors of Trio House Press would like to thank Chard deNiord.

Trio House Press, Inc. is dedicated to the promotion of poetry as literary art, which enhances the human experience and its culture. We contribute in an innovative and distinct way to American Poetry by publishing emerging and established poets, providing educational materials, and fostering the artistic process of writing poetry. For further information, or to consider making a donation to Trio House Press, please visit us online at: www.triohousepress.org.

Other Trio House Press Books you might enjoy:

Bird~Brain by Matt Mauch, 2017

Dark Tussock Moth by Mary Cisper
    2016 Trio Award Winner selected by Bhisham Bherwani

Break the Habit by Tara Betts, 2016

Bone Music by Stephen Cramer
    2015 Louise Bogan Award selected by Kimiko Hahn

*Rigging a Chevy into a Time Machine and Other Ways
    to Escape a Plague* by Carolyn Hembree
    2015 Trio Award Winner selected by Neil Shepard

Magpies in the Valley of Oleanders by Kyle McCord, 2015

Your Immaculate Heart by Annmarie O'Connell, 2015

The Alchemy of My Mortal Form by Sandy Longhorn
    2014 Louise Bogan Winner selected by Carol Frost

What the Night Numbered by Bradford Tice
    2014 Trio Award Winner selected by Peter Campion

Flight of August by Lawrence Eby
    2013 Louise Bogan Winner selected by Joan Houlihan

The Consolations by John W. Evans
    2013 Trio Award Winner selected by Mihaela Moscaliuc

Fellow Odd Fellow by Steven Riel, 2013

Clay by David Groff
    2012 Louise Bogan Winner selected by Michael Waters

Gold Passage by Iris Jamahl Dunkle
    2012 Trio Award Winner selected by Ross Gay

If You're Lucky Is a Theory of Mine by Matt Mauch, 2012